T0106501

Just You Alone

Victor Akinrinmade

authorHOUSE®

AuthorHouse™
1663 Liberty Drive
Bloomington, IN 47403
www.authorhouse.com
Phone: 1-800-839-8640

© 2012 Victor Akinrinmade. All rights reserved.

No part of this book may be reproduced, stored in a retrieval system, or transmitted
by any means without the written permission of the author.

Published by AuthorHouse 3/8/2012

ISBN: 978-1-4685-6126-5 (e)
ISBN: 978-1-4685-6002-2 (sc)

Library of Congress Control Number: 2012904217

Any people depicted in stock imagery provided by Thinkstock are models,
and such images are being used for illustrative purposes only.
Certain stock imagery © Thinkstock.

This book is printed on acid-free paper.

Because of the dynamic nature of the Internet, any web addresses or links contained in this book may have changed
since publication and may no longer be valid. The views expressed in this work are solely those of the author and do
not necessarily reflect the views of the publisher, and the publisher hereby disclaims any responsibility for them.

Table of Contents

My Beauty in Love

The way you are,
the way you smile
makes me wonder what
to do my dear.

A rose in red;
a rose in blue;
and a rose in white
will make a rhyme.

My love,
my dear,
my beauty in love;
what could I say to
win your soul?

I hold your hand;
you hold mine too
and the golden ring
begins to roll.

I love the way you
shine in light
and kissing you is a
food for thought.

I'm hungry my love;
I'm hungry my dear;
and I can't have
enough of you.

The Time but Goes

Make me come through,
come join me through;
and what a join that
would be my dear.

All the way the time
but goes, and I wonder
what to say my love.

The wonder story of
life is come, and I
know it's come to stay.

How the wonder would
be my love;

How we start, sometime
but now.

We would go a long
way dear, and together
we stand my love.

Make me come through;
join me come through;

and together we make
a match.

Victor Akinrinmade

Ring Me, My Love

Ring me tonight;
ring me, my dear
and tell me the little
juicy things of love.

I folded my hands,
and frown my face,
but you know the
secret of it my
love.

Give me a wink;
give me a smile,
give me the little
things that makes but
love.

Oh my dear love,
can you dig it?

The angle crossed;
the angle bent;
and the angle that reveals
the secret of love.

Ring me tonight;
ring me, my love
and I promise to
ring you too.

The Fact of Life

When I see the dove
flies off to sky, I but wonders
what to say my dear.

I love to see the dove
flies in and bring me
all the love I need.

The fact of life,
the hopes of days,
it rings the bell
as it tells me facts.

My darling one,
renew the joy,
the joy of living
and now and then.

The dove flies off as
hope seems gone but
flying in, the hope
renews.

My darling one,
my loving one,
the joy of living
is come to stay.

As the dove flies in,
the hope renews,
and what a wonder this
brings my love.

The Smile That Rose

The smile that rose to
me tonight, is the light
I yearned to see all day.

What did you say?

What did you hear?

As I want to know
you in and out.

I rise to the shining
day oh dear my love;
as hope in the spring
always flowers my dear.

The smile that rose
to me tonight is the
smile that will make the
days to come, my love.

Since hope and life
mingles so my dear;
as you will see in the
days to come.

Capturing the light;
capturing the day;
as I capture the
one I love.

As Time Goes On

Never give up hope my
dear; as the words
but rings its bell
my love.

You wonder on;
you wonder why;
the clouds so dark
sometimes, my love.

The fact of life is
that ray will show
after a bitter darken
night.

My loving one,
the fact is true;

we will make a smile
as the time goes on.

Never give up hope
my darling one,
since hope and need
moves hand in hand.

The fact of life is
this I know, that you
will make it as time
goes on.

Give Me a Kiss

Smiling and smiling
the way but goes,
as the brighten day
will make a walk.

The time is ripe,
the day but young,
all hopes and done
will make a talk.

My loving dear,
my loving one;
can we talk it,
the talk of hope?

When the hope seems
gone sometimes my
dear, is the breaking

of the dawn my dear.

The truth is this,
we will but smile,
at the breaking of
the day my dear.

Give me a kiss,
a kiss of love;
since the only hope
is a hope in need.

Victor Akinrinmade

Making the Stand

How do you see this
my loving dear;
that hope in deed will
come to stay?

The fact of life,
the hopes of days,
the golden rule that
rules the day.

My darling one,
my loving one,
let's join our hands
in love my dear.

The beauty in red,
the beauty in blue;

and it looks great
in the beauty in white.

My sweet heart dear,
my darling one;
how great it is to look
so young.

As our hope is young,
as our hope is strong;
we will make the
stand in the difficult
times.

Time to Wake

When the time goes
on the way it does
as the time will ripe
the way it does.

I know that time will
make a smile because
you look at me in eye.

Tell me the truth my
darling one; when do
the time goes ripe for
you?

The wondering light;
the wondering day,
the wondering sun but
makes a smile.

Tell me the truth
my darling one;
when do you get so
ripe for love?

I wonder on the way
I do,
that love will wake
everyone and me.

Victor Akinrinmade

The fact of life is this
my love;
it's time to wake
and ripe my love.

The Part That Leads

The way the part seems
glow my love;
is the roaming around the
way it does.

The part that moves my
head to yours, is the

the part that leads to
life my love.

Think it right dear;
think it right love
as we both think it with
heart so great, my dear.

The part I've never
known my dear is this
part of love my
darling one.

I strolled it through;
I walk it through
but the end only
smiled at me, my love.

Victor Akinrinmade

I love the way you
kiss my love;
as I love the way you
make me great.

In and out the ball
but rolls, as my darling
one will come but know.

The Butterfly Within

I feel the butterfly
within me oh
my love.

The way it moves, the way
it sings tells me your
love is there to last.

Oh my love, I would but
say that truth will but
win at last my dear.

Let's swing the love,
the love of hope;
since no water or
storm could quench
our love.

I still feel the butterfly
within me, my love;
as it keeps telling me

in a song so dear;
that love do stand
the test of time.

A kiss will do;
a romance will do,
and making love to

you will make me
arrive, oh my love;
my darling one.

Hopes of Our Yesterday

The romance of our yesterday
will touch today's my
love.

Let's swing in love
my darling one, since
hope and joy will
mingle through.

Kissing and touching
all but one, all rhymes
in love my darling one.

I wonder what to say
my dear, when the sun
looks so bright.

One thing is sure my
darling one, that
hope in spring and summer
joins to form the love
of time my dear.

Rolling and rolling,
the time would say
that even in tears
there is but
joy.

Victor Akinrinmade

I wonder what to say
my love, but you give
me the hopes of our
yesterday.

You Muses Me Love

What a scenery it is
my love, as we both
look from the decker bus.

You muses me love,
as you bury your head
in what you see.

On reading you through;
on reading your thoughts,
I can't but love you
more my love.

You blend with the
scene my love; as
your eyes shines with
the flow my dear.

Flowing and rising,
on it goes; it's nice
to seat on a
decker bus.

The river flows with
blending stream;
but the boats moves on
with rhyming flow.

Victor Akinrinmade

Without any ado,
I will but say, that
love makes a rhythm
for me.

The Way You Move

How green the grass,
how sweet it smells,
as a roaming light,
it just but glows.

Oh dear, my love,
oh dear, my own,
you look so fresh like
the green grass dear.

I love the looks
in your eyes my dear,
it is as pure as a
diamond in light.

How can I let you
know my love?

If you can read me
like a book my love;
you will then see I love
you true.

I love the way you
move your legs, whenever
you make your moves
my love.

Victor Akinrinmade

In all trueness, you
feed my soul, with
the kind of food only
you but know.

The winding up of the chapter
Is come;
I really love you true
my love.

Just Remember Me

The sky looks so bright
today my dear, and
the breeze is blowing
cool my love.

Do you remember our
yesterday my love,
and the walk on the
sea bank?

Do you remember the
sweet kisses, and love
making that rouse from
sky to falls?

How I love you
my dear;
how I need you;

an end I never see
my love.

Romancing you is a
food for thought,
my darling one
you got to know.

I keep the blanket warm
my love;
since loving you and
needing you, go hand in hand.

Whenever you remember
the yesterday, oh my love;
just remember that today
will only get better my dear.

The Fact is Come

What do you think
today, my dear?

An answering cloud
will make a bright.

The fact of life is this
my love to wink
at me is to kiss
my lips.

Where do we go from
here my love?

To know one thing is
to make a love.

Oh my darling one,
the fact is come;

the fact of life
is that I love you so.

When I kiss your hand,
Before you know, it comes
to your lips;
and on and on it goes.

Oh my darling one, I
love you so.

To ring the bell is
to wipe the tears;
and loving you my
words but say.

Bring Me a Smile

The day to remember
is this my love,
a loving day that comes
my way.

Let's talk it right,
let's smell it right,
as a loving smoke that
breaks the bound.

My loving one, I love
you so; and loving you
the way but be.

Give me a smile;
give me a talk,
since loving you will
raise my life.

Where do I go from
here my love?

The talking truth
is the talking words.

Bring me a smile my
loving one;
since loving you is
love indeed.

Victor Akinrinmade

The sky so bright,
the sun so shines,
and everything talk
my love for you.

Don't Worry Dear

The well is deep,
the rope is short,
I wonder how to get
through it my love.

My darling one, to
tell the truth, I
wonder how to get
through this.

Don't worry dear,
you said to me;
we join our ropes
together my love.

The rope of love,
the rope of joy;
the rope of eternity
fetching the water of life.

I know the love
joined hand to hand,
will move a mountain
like Everest, my dear.

Your love and mine,
joined hand to hand
will give us hopes
from life to life.

Victor Akinrinmade

When the Road Rolls

How can you say it,
when the road rolls;
the wondering part in
the way of man.

How can you say it
my loving dear;
as the road rolls on
and on my love.

The truth is this,
you speak the truth,
as love makes a
way where no way is.

I love you dear;
I need you dear;
as the road rolls on
the way it does.

Kissing and folding
all in love, will
never cease to stand
the test.

She stands the test
of time my love;
even as the road
rolls on.

Your Shining Smile

How glorious you are
my love;
your shining smile
melts the ice in cold.

Oh my darling one;
oh my gracious one;
you bring me hope in
the dark my love.

Let's talk it right,
let's move it right,
as a shining smile
will melt a heart.

My loving one;
my darling one;
how your smile but
moves me on.

I love you dear,
I need you dear,
and I love your shining
smile.

Victor Akinrinmade

Love Knows Us Well

Round and round it
flows away; as we
mingle through to the
higher ground.

Tell me the truth,
my darling one;
it seems that every
bird is got a nest
and the fox a hole
my loving one.

I tell you dear, this
is but true, that love
is the nest for
you and I.

The game of love is just
but sweet as
it flows from
head to toe.

The water of love is
so strange my love, since
it starts as a stream,
and end and endless sea.

Oh my love, let's swim in
love; let's live in love,
and let's dine in love
my dear.

Just as I know you
well; so does love
know us well my love.
She first finds us my dear.

When I Hold Your Hands

Run with me on the
grass lone my love,
and tell me all the
juicy little things that
spells out love.

Give me that lovely
look of yours my dear,
as I love to hold you
tight to myself
my love.

Do you know I love
you so;
do you,
my love,
do you?

Romancing and kissing
you are just the few of
many things I want to
do to you, my love.

Let's run on the grass
lone my love;
even the grass of love
my dear.

When I hold your hands
in mine; I will watch the
love flow through
us my dear.

How I love you,
my love I do.

When Love Rolls In

My dear should think
of the moment love glows;
even when the love
rolls in.

When the saying is
gone, and the parts
seems but gone;
then the part of love
will roll in my love.

I refuse to give up on
you my love; no matter
how clouded the day
might be, because

behind the thick whole
cloud is the shining light
my dear.

How I love you
my dear;
how I need you
my love.

Since love is stronger than
death my love, I know
that love will always rolls
us in, and when she does,
our part will shine.

My Love and Friend

My love, my friend;
my dear, and my smile,
how uniquely you make
me glow today.

Telling the truth my
loving one, I found no
word to quantify my
love for you.

You said you know;
you said you understand,
but can you look into
the sun and expect
not to be blinded
by it?

Oh my loved one,
if I open my heart
to you;

no horse and rider will stumble
passing through it,
my love.

You are my love and
friend my dear;
words that seldom
go together my love;
this you are to me,
my love.

Victor Akinrinmade

Our yesterday do
match with today,
and the story it tells
is that love is come
to stay my dear.

You Make Me Glow

My darling one, you
got to know that
as the light shines in
the dear old sun,
so do you make me
glow my love.

To think so bright,
to walk so tall,
is a way to shine
my love.

When I hold your hand
the way I do, I
but wonder where
to go next.

Do you know I
love you so my
dear?
Do you really know
how much I care?

Victor Akinrinmade

Thinking and rolling,
the bell will ring;
and when it does,
I will be there for
you my love.

How you make me
glow like the sun
my dear.

To Make a Smile

What do you think
today my love?

Where do you want
to go my dear?

To start with dear,
I love you so;
with no doubt dear,
I need you so.

Jumping the moon,
and jumping the sun;
what else to jump
to make a smile?

My loving one, I
seek a kiss;
as a long kiss dear
will be enough.

How I love you;
how I need you
as you bring a smile
to my soul my love.

Thank God, You Really Care

The way you look
at me in the picture
my love, makes me to
yearn for you and more.

I never know you
love me so, but a
naked eye can read
your soul.

You never know how
much you showed
that you love me
and me alone.

As the picture stands
on the shelf my

love, I never know
you love me so.

I used to think;
I used to yearn;
and I used to wish
you love me too.

Thank you for loving me
too, my love;
I thank God, you
really care my dear.

The Goal is Come

Round and round the
part but be; as a
winding road it just
but be.

The goal is come;
the part is real;
as you can but see
the part is true.

My darling one, this
one is true, that
the part to your heart
is mine to yours.

Draining the part that
seems but go; as you
can see the end is
good.

The goal is come;
the part is true, as
you will see my
darling one.

I love to think the
way I do and rhyme
the words with voice so
sweet.

Victor Akinrinmade

My darling one, the
part is come, the part
to my love for your
heart my dear.

Don't Cry for Me

Like a wondering life
my way but be;
as I wonder on the
part to go.

Don't cry for me, my
love I pray, 'cause
the part slippery today
will smooth I know.

Don't cry for me, my
darling one, for the
future is bright for
me for sure.

I wonder why this
part so rough, and
wonder still the part
to go.

Don't cry for me
'cause the future is
bright; as you will
see the way it be.

I still wonder what
to do my love;
and wonder still
the part to go.

Victor Akinrinmade

Hope with me my
love, please do I
pray, since hope indeed
is hope in life.

What a Pen It Is

My loving one, I've
got the gift; a loving
gift it is my love.

What a pen it is my
loving one; it writes
so fine within so sweet.

Let's talk of love,
let's talk of joy,
and let's talk of smile
that sinks so deep.

My loving one, the
pen is great; as you
will know, it writes
so nice.

What a pen this is,
what a love this is,
a golden pen
that writes so fine.

My darling one, the
words are true,
that love will win
the battle my love.

What a great pen,
what a great love,
the pen writes nice
with love so great.

I Will Meet You

What can I say,
what would I do to
make the drum but
glow my love?

The rising sun,
the rising tide,
and more and more
it goes that way.

My loving one, you've
got to know that the
tide of life it
seems but come.

Tell me the truth
my loving one,
do you see me
the way I do?

The fact of life is
this my love, that
I will meet you in
the tide of life.

The Candle Burns

The truth of life
is this I know that
the joy of life is
come my way.

My loving one,
my darling one,
the candle burns
as you just can see.

Oh my, I say;
the world seems slow,
how wonder on I
just must be.

My love, your eyes
are bright like star;
and I wonder the
way they do.

The fact of life,
the ways of life,
is the truth that mingles
the way they do.

Oh my dear love,
oh my dear one,
the candle burns so
bright my dear.

What Would I Say?

The rocking with
the rolling stone, is
one thing dear, I
won't forget.

The way you move,
the way you smile,
will rock me on and
more, my love.

To see the eyes that
makes me smile; seeing
the joy that bring me love,
is a laughter in mood my dear.

Oh mine, my dear;
oh mine, my love;
what would I say
to make you rock?

I love the move;
I love the waves;
I love the current that
you charge in me.

Victor Akinrinmade

The Rhyming Talk

Thinking the way you
are my love, is
one thing true I
won't forget.

The life that mingles
day with light, is the
only dream I want
to know.

My loving one;
my darling one;
the fact of life is
this I know.

Mingling the wind with
sky my love, is
love you bring into
my life, my dear.

The rhyming talk;
the smiling lips;
the joy of life is
the words to say.

My darling one;
you have to know,
you bring me joy as
the time goes - bye.

The Tunnel of Life

The firing blues;
the windy air;
the joy of life as
time goes - bye.

Where would I go
from here my dear?

Where would I go
my love?

I know the life of
day is bright, and
can seems dull
sometimes my love.

But in the tunnel
of life my dear;
one thing is sure,
that the spring of life
still drips my love.

Let's smile it one;
let's smile it through;
since the joy of life
stands the test
of time.

Victor Akinrinmade

The Kiss of Life

How wonderful it is
to me today;
the joy of life but
comes my way.

The kiss of life;
the bright of day;
the smile that wakes
me here and then.

Wondering where to
talk the life my dear;
I know you bring my
day and life.

The truth is this my
loving one, you wake
me on as days
goes – bye.

You push me here;
I push you there,
as the kiss of life breeds
the hopes we need.

Smile me through dear;
smile me through love;
smile me to the bottom
of hope my love.

Your Lips but Drips

I love your smile
as it sings the song;
the song of life and
on my dear.

I love your legs as
they swallow the ground;
it moves with waves
that last so long.

The truth of this
my darling one, is
that you glow with
inner joy.

I know that truth
will win at last;
but the truth of it is,
it's moves me on.

Your eyes tells me a
loving song; and
your lips but drips
with honey comb.

Oh my dear one;
oh my love one;
the fact of life is
a story indeed.

Victor Akinrinmade

An Arrow Shot

The water flows
around the life,
and what it says is
the joy is come.

Thinking the way
you whisper dear;
an arrow shot,
an arrow gone.

The water flows
the way it does,
and whisper love and
then it's gone.

My darling one;
my loving one;
the gap is bridged
as life goes on.

Thinking and whispering,
the day will come,
as your beauty glows
reminds me of love.

Life will say it;
life will think it;
and life will make
the day come true.

You Bring Me Joy

What a day this is
my love, 'cause you
bring my joy today
my dear.

I roaming round the
clock my dear, and
what I see makes
me smile, my love.

You bring me joy and
then you smiled; for
oh my love you
know me well.

Kissing your lips,
folding you to me
is one thing dear
I won't forget.

You bring me life,
my darling one,
and what it says is
that love have come.

Sweet darling one;
sweet loving one;
I just want you to
know I love you so.

When hope seems
gone; when life seems
dead; it is the time
that love will glow.

Smile Again

Smile my love, please
smile, as you will
see, your hope
is come.

Smile again my love,
I say, for hope denied
is hope indeed; as it
comes your way it comes indeed.

My darling one, you
just must know, that
life renewed it's hope
from life to life.

Smile again, my darling
one, 'cause a hope
denied will come
alive.

Telling the truth
my darling one, that
joy do come when
the dawn breaks through.

My darling one, my
loving one; the fact
of life is to know
the truth.

Victor Akinrinmade

The way to life
is to smile again; and
when you do, you will
break the ice.

Let's Roam the Stars

Don't give up dear,
you don't forget
for the round table
is strong my love.

The turning wheel,
the swelling well, as
it rise from day to
day my glowing love.

Think it today,
think it my dear,
and think it my
joy, as you come afar.

Sink it so well,
sink it too good,
and sink it so bright,
my loving dear.

Let's roam the stars;
let's roam the seas,
and let's roam the
globe my darling one.

You know the truth,
you know me well,
as the stars do the
twinkling oh my love.

Victor Akinrinmade

Let's roam the land;
let's roam the seas,
and let's roam the
stars my loving dear.

Blow Me a Kiss

What can I say today
my love?

Can the day sing the
song of night?

The fact of life is this
I know, that the talk
of life is come to
stay.

Oh my loved one;
oh my dear one,
tell me the truth
as we walk for life.

My darling one, the
truth is come, that
the way of life will
come anew.

Blow me a kiss;
blow me your love,
and blow me the joy
that come with love.

The fact of life is
this my love, as truth
will win as time
goes on.

Blow me a kiss,
blow me your love,
blow me a day as
bright as the sun.

The Day I Grew Up

A vegetable into a tree
is eternity to me I know;
but waking up one morning
and I was grown up.

Tell me day light;
tell me dear moon,
why is it you never
change?
As ever, you make forget
my days.

Like flowing stream
that flows away,
my life is passing
me bye and bye.

What would I say?
What would I do?
I see my today
passing me bye.

It never care what I
do with my life but
just rolling and
rolling away.

I remember the day
I was young;
eternity is growing up;
but like a dream I
woke up from sleep
to find my time
is gone.

Why do you prove me
wrong my day?
Like a fading dream
you are to me;

and my destiny is
already planned.
tell me dear light;
tell me dear moon;

'cause I was young
but now I'm old,
but you never but
seems to change.

When to Come In

The sound is hot,
I'm wet all through
but won't let
me in my love.

Waiting and waiting,
time can't bear, but
my love for you is
all I know.

My soul tells me
I must wait for you;
but waiting, my
heart can't bear.

When will you go
ripe my love?
When will you know,
my love?

The streams of water
flows away, my eyes
looks on as it
fades away.

Love and patience go
hand in hand, but
the bitter truth is to
wait for it.

Victor Akinrinmade

When should I come
in my love?

When would you open
your door for me?

Oh God in heaven
knows my heart;
the heart that wait
all this time for you.

I know the time
will come my love,
when you would be
ripe for me, and I
will be there for
you.

The Girls from the Blue

It's just but true,
it's just but well;
the four girls from
the blue.

Once I met them,
a team they form,
a day so blue and
bright.

I wonder what to
call their names,
I still can't make
my mind.

One was as quiet
as a moving ball;
another talks like
me.

She looked at me
with a dancing eyes,
and only smiled
at me.

They make a team;
they formed a team;
the four girls from
the blue.

The Prince

The happiest man I
know is him and
very humbled too;
he goes to war with

few and back with
plenty;
wisdom rose like
a tower hill,

fame goes far and
wide. How his subjects
takes to is
bow.

The fear of God makes
him so wise, and
rich in wealth and
fame.

The best of life he
thought his own, and
he never misuse his
power.

His people think their
prince is wise;
for me, for me,
I think it too.

The House Peter Built

This is the house
which Peter Built;
the rat can pass,
the mouse can talk;

and Peter is strong
and good.
The house of hay,
the roof of plank,

but little Peter
cannot get in.
Oh see the tears;
oh see the cry,

the mood of Peter
cannot be said.
But the rat can talk;
The mouse can leap;

They want to thank
Peter for the house
Well built; but Peter
Just sat and wept.

Truth is Bitter in Truth

The truth is bitter in
truth, so says a sage
in town.

Oh man,
oh man, you see,
you see them
throw their stones
at the old and wearied
man who just but
said the truth.

The truth is bitter
I know; but how many
Can say it?

But look the soul of
man who speaks
the truth always;
the Lord looks

down at him and
makes a smile at him.
The best of his chariot
he send to take

his soul up home.
His soul can't waste
in sand; the Lord
can't bear it once.

The Lord is lonely
for him;
the Lord just want
his kiss.

Tears never fall from
his eyes again; he
lives more and more,
never to die again.

Victor Akinrinmade

Never to Have a Friend

Never to have a
friend 'cause is not
good for me.

Never to have a friend
who laughs at your folly,
and never let you know.

Never to have a friend
who makes a fun of you,
and makes a fool of you.

Never to have a friend
who conspires against
you and laughs to
your face.

What need is a friend,
if he brings me nothing
but grieves and
faints?

Friends Making a Fight

The friend in need;
the friend indeed.

What band never
quarrelled and never
regroup again?

They think it good,
they think it bad,
two sheep still join
a fight.

She makes the shout;
he makes the bow,
and both feeling so
great.

He took her in;
she took him out,
but my own friends
can make a fight.

The Rolling Rock

The rolling rock;
the rolling storm,
the tiger in haste
runs for its fray.

I'm at home;
I'm at sea,
counting the eggs,
and they are still firm.

I count them once;
I count them twice,
about a third time,
and never made a blast.

I think it wise,
I think it best
that the bag of
faults is still alive.

My fun goes high,
my fun goes low,
but thanks to God
that I'm alive.

The State Fair

I'm going to the
state fair,
the state fair,
the state fair.

The city gate is
open, and flying
a bit high.

He was so strong
as iron,
he was as good
as gold.

The king threw his
golden crown,
the horse made a
pick.

I can just make
a fly on earth,
and make a jump on
moon.

I'm going to the
state fair,
the state fair I
would be.

Victor Akinrinmade

Without My Failures

Failure as many
think it is a strong
way to doom they
know.

But what a story
she tells to me;
she is always a
stepping stone.

Many fear her sting,
and many when
she knocks at their
door.

But how many successful
individuals have never
drank from her
cup?

Kings and princes eat
from her table.

But thanks to my failures;
I would never
have known my
faults.

What a Couple

What a couple,
what a pair?
And love the ring
that fixed the day.

In my few days
I'm yet to see,
a love as strong as
fire.

With God's kind
hand leading the
way, I'm sure the
future is bright.

And hello, my
Lovely;

a honeymoon on a
tree house?

Examination

Examination is like
running a race;
the sport man picks
his challenge;

from the start
and make his stand
all through.

Getting near the tape,
he gets very tired
but he just have
to get to the end.

How he would make it,
that is no question;
the energy in him
he uses very well.

He runs and passes
the tape so well;
how people shout at
his victory.

And alas,
he made it up!

From Youth I Grow

From youth I grow
and grew so strong
with pretty nature
surrounding me.

I sleep at night,
I woke at day,
and thanking the Lord,
I'm good as new.

Mummy is there,
daddy is there,
and all my beloved
ones.

In terrible states
I always be due
to all my foolish
wants.

God is always there,
he is always there,
always to comfort
the foolish child.

I love it much;
I love him much,
but I don't know
how to thank him much.

Victor Akinrinmade

The Man You Knew

What do you think
of life oh man,
how do you think
of life?

The man you knew
so well is dead,
and what about
his dreams?

He can't speak
for himself again;
but will is character
speak for him?

I look the world
so wide and round,
and what can replace
a soul my dear?

My God, my all,
my creator in youth,
I want your breath
so near.

You help me live
my life today,
and the few days
down ahead.

The Love of Man

The love of man is
all he knows;
I can't but have
a say.

As man compared,
is just but little
mess.

He sings is song,
he makes a noise
and blow the sky
all off!

But real love is
just too true;
it's just too good
and calm;
it got its source
from God.

But man's way
always right;
he knows nothing
but more.

Make Me Your King

Your love is shaking
me like a tree;
you make me your king
is all I ask;
and I promise you
be my queen.

Let the world know,
let the world see
what a king you made
of me;

and I will let
her know what a
queen you are
my love.

Never Happened Before

It shook the wall,
it shook the king,
it's never happen before.
He did what no man
has done;
he saw what no man
has seen.

The king will have a
feast!
Call in the beauties;
call in the lovers;
bring Isreal's vessels
and let them
drink!

Praise the iron,
praise the gold,
let us cheer to our
great king's feast.

But like a light
the colour changed;
a strange hand is writing
on the wall.

Your kingdom is come
to an end, oh king;
weighted and
found wanting.

Victor Akinrinmade